More of Jesus...

...Less of Me!

By
DAVID MAYORGA

SHABAR PUBLICATIONS
www.shabarpublications.com

Most Shabar Publications products are available at special quantity discounts for bulk purchase for sales promotions, fund-raising and educational needs. For details, write Shabar Publications at mayorga1126@gmail.com.

More of Jesus...Less of Me! by David Mayorga

Published by Shabar Publications
3833 N. Taylor Rd.
Palmhurst, Texas 78573
www.shabarpublications.com

This book or parts thereof may not be reproduced in any form, stored in a retrieval system, or transmitted in any form by any means - electronic, mechanical, photocopy, recording, or otherwise - without prior written permission of the publisher, except as provided by United States of America copyright law.

Unless otherwise noted, all Scripture quotations are from the New Kings James Version of the Bible. Copyright@1979, 1980, 1982 by Thomas Nelson, Inc., publishers. Used by permission.

Copyright@2025 by David Mayorga
All rights reserved.

ISBN 978-1-955433-30-3

Note: This publication contains the opinions and ideas of its author(s). It is intended to provide helpful and informative material on the subject matter covered. It is sold with the understanding that the author(s) and publisher are not engaged in rendering professional service in the book. If the reader requires personal assistance or advice, a competent professional should be consulted. The author(s) and publisher specifically disclaim any responsibility for any liability, loss, or risk, personal or otherwise, which is incurred as a consequence, directly or indirectly, of the use and application of any of the contents of this book.

"Who may ascend into the hill of the LORD?
Or who may stand in His holy place?
He who has clean hands and a pure heart,
Who has not lifted his soul to an idol,
Nor sworn deceitfully.
He shall receive blessing from the LORD,
And righteousness from the God of his salvation.
This is Jacob, the generation of those who seek Him,
Who seek Your face."

(Psalm 24:3-6)

Table of Content

Break Our Hearts (lyrics) 4

Dedication 6

Introduction 8

Chapter 1: Humility As Lived Out By Jesus! 14

Chapter 2: No Reserves, No Regrets, No Retreats! 20

Chapter 3: Leave the Fish! 32

Chapter 4: The Real You: Recognizing the Latent Power of Self & Sin! 40

Chapter 5: Job: I Will Still Worship! 53

Chapter 6: The True Friends of God 66

Chapter 7: Stay Focused With God's Plan 73

Chapter 8: Face to Face! 83

Chapter 9: Leaning! 92

Chapter 10: "Mold Me Until It Seems Good to You, Oh God!" 100

Conclusion: "I Don't Want to Be Anything Big!" 109

Break Our Hearts

Teach us, O Lord, what it really means,
To rend our hearts instead of outer things.
Teach us, O God, what we do not see,
About our hearts and of Your ways.

And Father deal with our carnal desires,
To move in Your power but not live the life.
To love our neighbors with all that we have,
And keep our tongues from saying things we have not seen.

Oh, break our hearts with the things that break Yours.
What we sow in tears, we will reap in joy.
That we might pass through Your refining fire
Where brokenness awaits on the other side.

Raise up an army like Joel saw,
Your church is stronger than ever before.
They will not break ranks when they plunge through the fences,
The fear of the Lord will be their wisdom.

That they might weep as Jesus wept,
A fountain of tears for the wounded and lost,
Whoever heard of an army O God,
That conquered the earth -
by weeping and mourning and brokenness?

There will be a day when the nations will bow,
And the Lord will be King over all the earth,
He will be the only One,
and also, His name will be the only One.

Save Us, Oh God!
Vineyard Music (1990)

Dedication

This book is dedicated to all who have made Jesus Lord and King! To the countless servants of God who have set their hearts like flint to pursue the majesty and fullness of Christ. To all those who have positioned their lives to be used by the Spirit of God, not counting their lives, even unto death. The dedication also goes to those who have shut themselves in the secret place of prayer and intercession through countless sleepless nights until Christ is formed in the generation that is to come. These are the servants who have learned the secrets of God's heart and have willfully given themselves to discover the Father's wishes and who, with the same spirit as the Apostle Paul, agree with him saying, **"But what things were gain to me, these**

I have counted loss for Christ. Yet indeed I also count all things loss for the excellence of the knowledge of Christ Jesus my Lord, for whom I have suffered the loss of all things, and count them as rubbish, that I may gain Christ and be found in Him, not having my own righteousness, which is from the law, but that which is through faith in Christ, the righteousness which is from God by faith; that I may know Him and the power of His resurrection, and the fellowship of His sufferings, being conformed to His death, if, by any means, I may attain to the resurrection from the dead." (Philippians 3:7-11)

To close this dedication, I want to thank God for all the men and women of God whom I have had the privilege of meeting around the world and who, without their knowing, have profoundly impacted me; also, I might add, to all those who have lived their lives not only unselfishly but fully surrendered and yielded to the will of God, even when it was not convenient.

Lastly, thank you for your perseverance as the standard of life in Christ. Numerous times, it was easier to pack it up, give up, and go home—but you didn't! Thank you for showing the way of the cross!

- David Mayorga, *Author*

Introduction

As I worshipped the Lord during the worship time at Oasis (the church where we minister in Matamoros, Tamaulipas, Mexico) - the Spirit of the Lord caused me to ponder the thoughts written in the book of John where Jesus is at the feast. This story is found in John 7:37, 38: **"On the last day, that great day of the feast, Jesus stood and cried out, saying, "If anyone thirsts, let him come to Me and drink. He who believes in Me, as the Scripture has said, out of his heart will flow rivers of living water." But this He spoke concerning the Spirit, whom those believing in Him would receive…"**.

Jesus said that if anyone at any place and time believed, out of their belly would flow rivers of living water—not just one river but many rivers! This is God's design: that all who come to Him would never thirst again for the things of earth, for He would be full satisfaction and full joy to all who would enter.

If He is living waters, why do we drink from other cisterns? If He has put rivers within us, why are we not content? Why do we continually seek to drink from other cisterns rather than be fulfilled in Christ alone?

Perhaps we have not tasted the Lord's goodness or have caught a glimpse of the Lord's presence in our lives. Maybe we are still trying to please the flesh: selfish ambitions, carnal desires, or we are pursuing personal aggrandizement.

When the rivers are flowing, there is no longing for anything else but for more of that glory. Through my walk and journey with God, I have discovered that the real battle in our soul begins when we lose sight of His presence. Without a touch of His manifest presence, our lives sink into the mire of fleshly desire. When this happens, our lives begin to look for substitutes!

Once we lose sight of the revelation that Christ is all we need, that it is Christ alone who fills our all and all, we begin to substitute with our hands what we lose in our soul. Here's where I believe the trap of self (flesh) taking control starts to take root.

When we lose touch with God, material things become the attraction!

When Christ is no longer the priority, we stop drawing near to Him. If, at one time, Christ's words to you were meaningful, they no longer hold your attention. Something has transpired, and now we will look for applause and approval from men rather than God; we long for fame, status, and reputation rather than to have our identity found in Christ alone.

After the Apostle Peter was filled with the Spirit, he found his identity in Christ. He wrote some of the most descriptive and beautiful words, **"But you are a chosen generation, a royal priesthood, a holy nation, His own special people, that you may proclaim the praises of Him who called you out of darkness into His marvelous light; who once were not a people but are now the people of God, who had not obtained mercy but now have obtained mercy."** (1 Peter 2:9, 10)

As I continued in worship, pondering all that the Spirit of God was saying to my heart, the words from John 3:30 became increasingly loud. John the Baptist said, **"He must increase, but I must decrease."**

If there is anything we can take away from John the Baptist and the powerful Spirit-led life he lived, it is this: He quickly pointed to Christ, the Lord. In essence, John was saying, I am not alive today for my sake; my life is about promoting the life of Jesus -nothing else! John adds by saying, I indeed baptize you with water; but One mightier than I is coming, whose sandal strap I am not worthy to lose. He will baptize you with the Holy Spirit and fire.

In the following chapters, God has put in my heart a few principles about what it means to desire more of Christ's characteristics and how one must enter a life of deeper brokenness. To have more of Jesus, one must die more to self. There is no way around this. I hear believers crying out, Jesus, give me more of You! I can almost hear Jesus saying, You, give me more of you, and you will have more of Me!

More of Jesus, Less of Me! has been written to lift the hungry servant of Jesus to a higher ground in the knowledge of Christ, producing a deeper impact on him and on those who hear Him. To God be the glory now and forever! Enjoy.

1

Humility as Lived Out By Jesus!

Let this same attitude and purpose and [humble] **mind be in you which was in Christ Jesus:** [Let Him be your example in humility:] **Who, although being essentially one with God and in the form of God** [possessing the fullness of the attributes which make God God], **did not think this equality with God was a thing to be eagerly grasped or retained, But stripped Himself** [of all privileges and rightful dignity], **so as to assume the guise of a servant (slave), in that He became like men and was born a human being. And after He had appeared in human form, He abased and humbled Himself** [still further] **and carried**

His obedience to the extreme of death, even the death of the cross! Therefore [because He stooped so low] **God has highly exalted Him and has freely bestowed on Him the name that is above every name, That in (at) the name of Jesus every knee should (must) bow, in heaven and on earth and under the earth, and every tongue** [frankly and openly] **confess and acknowledge that Jesus Christ is Lord, to the glory of God the Father.**" (Philippians 2:5-11 *Amplified Version*)

After learning about Christ's life of brokenness, we would do well to explore the idea or philosophy of brokenness, its origin, and how one can maintain this life that pleases God's heart.

If you allow me to share the revelation written in my heart and how this manuscript came to fruition, I will attempt to teach how I believe a life of brokenness works and how God's servants lived in such a way that it made such a powerful impact.

God's Attitude, Purpose, and Mind for His Servants.

In the Amplified Version, in the letter to the Philippians, the Apostle Paul brought to light an interesting subject – the philosophy behind the life of Christ.

He starts by saying, **"Let this same attitude and purpose and** [humble] **mind be in you which was in Christ Jesus:** [Let Him be your example in humility:]" Regarding humility, Christ would be our poster child, no doubt! Jesus, the King of the Universe, taught us what humility is.

Humility affects our attitude, our purpose, and our mind. When we understand humility from Christ's perspective, a life of obedience makes a lot of sense.

For starters, let me lay out a few definitions of humility. The Cambridge Dictionary defines humility as the feeling or attitude that you have no special importance that makes you better than others, lack of pride. The Collins Dictionary says, "Someone who has humility is not proud and does not believe they are better than others.

I personally define humility as the attitude, purpose, and mindset of putting God first in everything!

Jesus Willfully Humbled Himself While in Heaven!

Humility is the attitude and way of life in heaven. All creation bows before the Father and carries out His wishes at any time and place. In other words, all creation's purpose is to bring God pleasure in all things.

As the Father needed to send His Son Jesus to earth, I don't believe there was a struggle in Jesus's life. I don't think Jesus was pleading with the Father and saying, I don't want to go to earth! I don't want to leave all my glory! Please, Father, please, don't send me. I don't believe it went down like that.

I believe God called on His Son to come to earth, and He willfully and readily came to bring the Father pleasure. Anything You need me to do, Father, I'll do it! said the heart of Jesus.

When serving God, one must do it for God's sake—not for man or any special interest but for God and God alone—to please Him! Obedience out of a heart of humility brings pleasure to our heavenly Father.

Here's what we must learn: Humility is the nature of Christ. If we can't grasp this, we will have a hard time obeying any of His commands. God must always be first.

If God's servant learns to walk in humility before God, he will not have trouble walking in humility before man.

When one walks in this wisdom, our kingdom of heaven priorities will be carried out without fighting the Holy Spirit's promptings. The unyielding heart has difficulty obeying and pleasing the Father's heart.

Jesus Willfully Humbled Himself While on Earth!

"Who, although being essentially one with God and in the form of God [possessing the fullness of the attributes which make God God], **did not think this equality with God was a thing to be eagerly grasped or retained…".**

Before a man or woman of God can truly walk and serve Jesus, the servant must lay His life down so Christ can flow unhindered through him.

Could Jesus have made an argument and said, "I am one with God; therefore, I have rights. I have the right to use my attributes of God and defend myself from any harm coming my way?" Of course, He could have argued his way out of anything that made demands upon His life, but He chose not to!

Living for Jesus is Never About Our Will But His!

The Scriptures say that Jesus said, **"For I have come down from heaven, not to do My own will, but the will of Him who sent Me."** (John 6:38)

Once totally yielded to the Father's wishes, Jesus took up the Father's will and declared it to all: I am not here on earth for Me but for My Father!

We must remember that as a priority, you and I are here by and for God's will!

Unless a man or woman who has been born-again lays down their life for the sake of Christ, they will not be able to please the Father.

Here's the formula that Jesus gave . . .

He Stripped Himself!

Instead of exalting Himself, He did the opposite. Listen to this: **"But stripped Himself** [of all privileges and rightful dignity]**, so as to assume the guise of a servant (slave), in that He became like men and was born a human being. And after He had appeared in human form, He abased and humbled Himself** [still further] **and carried His obedience to the extreme of death, even the death of the cross!**

Interestingly, Jesus didn't need anyone to tell Him what His place was. He knew He had come from God and could have avoided the pain, struggle, hate, threats, and anguish at any

given moment—but He didn't! Scripture clearly states that Jesus stripped Himself of all privileges and rightful dignity. His willful choice was to become a servant, a slave, and pay the price required by a just God, which included taking obedience to the extreme of death on a cross!
The Reward of the Faithful Is

"**Therefore** [because He stooped so low] **God has highly exalted Him and has freely bestowed on Him the name that is above every name…**".

One thing I have noticed about earthly rewards is that people always serve in the world with a condition attached: they get paid for what they do. Isn't this the standard of worldly systems?

If the price is right, people will do something for Jesus. Will this be recognized by the church board, members, leaders, pastors, etc.? People who are true servants—serve! This includes putting in the time, the money, the gifting, and then some! Serving is about sacrifice. It's about living simply so others can simply live!

My pastor used to say the rewards of God are out of this world!

When we humbly serve God, the Lord will ensure our value increases. God is a good bookkeeper and will keep tabs on everything we do, flowing out of a humble and contrite heart. Nothing beats the promotion that only God can give!

2

No Reserves, No Regrets, No Retreats!

From that time Jesus began to show to His disciples that He must go to Jerusalem, and suffer many things from the elders and chief priests and scribes, and be killed, and be raised the third day. Then Peter took Him aside and began to rebuke Him, saying, "Far be it from You, Lord; this shall not happen to You!" But He turned and said to Peter, "Get behind Me, Satan! You are an offense to Me, for you are not mindful of the things of God, but the things of men." (Matthew 16:21-23)

I want to open this chapter by saying that the Christian lifestyle, as practiced by our early forefathers, differs from the life practiced today in most Christian circles. Christianity today has been taught with an American or Western cultural ideology. It's a Christianity that propagates self and outward blessing rather than an inward blessing.

The pursuit of materialism and security seems to be the order of the day, and preachers in today's pulpits ensure that this message is taught and preached in their churches. Is it any wonder that believers today live very shallow spiritual lives and, as a result, live in shambles?

Mindful of the Things of Men!

As Jesus made the circuit, healing people and preaching the Good News of the kingdom, He began to open himself up more and more to those closest to Him, His disciples.

As He began to share what the future would look like regarding Himself, Peter took Him aside and began rebuking Him. Picture this! "Far be it from You, Lord; this shall not happen to You." It was Peter's way of saying, "I am not allowing no one to take you to no cross – Jesus, you are not dying!"

As noble and as sincere the words spoken by Peter were, it was the flesh speaking! It was Peter's fleshly desires attempting to look for its interest. I have often wondered how often we have defended our position, purpose, vision, family, ministry, or business to say that "God wouldn't allow that in my life!"

Listen to the words of Jesus: **"Get behind Me, Satan! You are an offense to Me, for you are not mindful of the things of God, but the things of men."**

The word **offense** here means *to tie a noose or to set a trap.*

This was Jesus' way of saying to Peter, you are trying to trap Me, Peter, by allowing your flesh to govern you! Your flesh only thinks of self. It can't think of God's interests!

My Two Natures!

In the Christian faith, one thing to know is that there is one of you with two natures. The Spirit that lives and cohabitates with your spirit after you have been born-again, and the fleshly part of you that was inherited from birth.

Galatians says, **"But I say, walk and live** [habitually] **in the** [Holy] **Spirit** [responsive to and controlled and guided by the Spirit]; **then you will certainly not gratify the cravings and desires of the flesh (of human nature without God).**

For the desires of the flesh are opposed to the [Holy] Spirit, and the [desires of the] **Spirit are opposed to the flesh (godless human nature); for these are antagonistic to each other** [continually withstanding and in conflict with each other], **so that you are not free but are prevented from doing what you desire to do."** (Galatians 5:16, 17 *Amplified Version*)

Anyone who has been a believer for a short time knows that a constant battle is being waged daily. The spirit and the flesh are daily in conflict from the minute you wake up to the minute you go to sleep. If you remain in this human body, you will have conflict!

Now, this journey with God boils down to choices. We must choose His will or else be enslaved by our own will.

No Reserves!

"Then Jesus said to His disciples, If anyone desires to be My disciple, let him deny himself [disregard, lose sight of, and forget himself and his own interests] **and take up his cross and follow Me** [cleave steadfastly to Me, conform wholly to My example in living and, if need be, in dying, also]. **For whoever is bent on saving his** [temporal] **life** [his comfort and security here] **shall lose it** [eternal life];

and whoever loses his life [his comfort and security here] **for My sake shall find it** [life everlasting]." (Matthew 16:24, 25. -*Amplified Version*)

When a believer comes to Christ, the first thing He must realize and come to terms with is how horrible and wicked self is! Self has an agenda – to steal away your destiny in God.

It is not only hard but impossible to disregard, lose sight of, and forget your interests in your own power. To embrace Christ fully, one must come to the end of self. Here's where the rubber meets the road!

You see, everyone can go to church, to a cell group, or a bible study, but not all want to go to the cross to die. You cannot cleave steadfastly to Christ, conform wholly to His example in living, and even die for Him if you have not died to self!

Now, if you have died to self and are cleaving steadfastly to Him, you will hear the heartbeat of worship and service to Him so clearly.

No Regrets!

"**And while He was in Bethany,** [a guest] **in the house of**

Simon the leper, as He was reclining [at table], **a woman came with an alabaster jar of ointment (perfume) of pure nard, very costly and precious; and she broke the jar and poured** [the perfume] **over His head. But there were some who were moved with indignation and said to themselves, To what purpose was the ointment (perfume) thus wasted? For it was possible to have sold this** [perfume] **for more than 300 denarii** [a laboring man's wages for a year] **and to have given** [the money] **to the poor. And they censured and reproved her. But Jesus said, Let her alone; why are you troubling her? She has done a good and beautiful thing to Me** [praiseworthy and noble]." (Mark 14:3-6. -*Amplified Version*)

In Spirit and Truth!

While studying worship, I realized you cannot access the throne room unless the Spirit of God invites you to worship.

Unless the Spirit of God initiates the desire to worship, you can't come. Many people come, but they have not been invited. So, they sing songs and give offerings out of carnal instinct, not by spiritual invitation.

Many have tried to serve God in the flesh (intellect). They

think they can help God by doing good works, for they feel capable, smart, gifted, or moved by compassion. Let me say that **"Unless the Lord builds the house, they labor in vain who build it."** (Psalm 127:1)

The Costly Perfume!

The fact that the woman who came to pour her perfume before Jesus didn't care how much the gift was, tells you much about true worship.

To give something to the Lord that is of high value to you - speaks volumes of the condition of that man or woman's heart.

She felt that offering Christ this perfume was her best and that He was worth it all and much more, so she paid Him and the disciples a visit. When she got to where Jesus was sitting, she broke the jar (which was very expensive), poured the anointing oil of spikenard (also very expensive), and anointed the head of Jesus!

One thing to notice in true worship is this: We do it with all our hearts; we don't bring anything back! When the woman gave the very expensive perfume, she broke the jar; she wasn't bringing any perfume back home. This is what I call living a life with no regrets! It's a one-way ticket to the heart of Jesus! Are you living this way?

Why This Waste?

In contemplating this woman's act, I don't believe that her act of worship violated anything deserving of condemnation and criticism. The woman was the proud owner of an alabaster jar of costly perfume, which she had probably been saving for that great event. She discovered the Great Event—it was Jesus, the Messiah!

There were some people there who thought it was a big waste of such costly oil, and they were upset, saying, you are just going to throw it away on the head of Jesus...come on! What a waste!

This group of naysayers is nothing more than the expression of flesh in us. You see, we all like to give because it is a noble thing to do. But often, we only give until it truly costs us something! When this begins to happen, we pull back. We must discern this.

Let us look at this woman; she gave the costliest thing she

owned.

I pray that God will take us to that next level of giving with no regrets!

No Retreats!

One characteristic of a true follower of Jesus is that the servant doesn't give up or quit. The Spirit of the Lord leads him and knows exactly what God needs him or her to do.

Anyone can say they love Jesus when things are going well, but will they feel the same about Jesus when things are going bad?

Once and for all, we must decide if Christ is the one we want to follow. The journey will get rough sometimes, but we must know this is the way!

If Jesus (while on Earth) decided to please the Father, you and I will have to do the same and choose!

"The Lord GOD has given Me
The tongue of the learned,
That I should know how to speak
A word in season to him who is weary.

He awakens Me morning by morning,
He awakens My ear
To hear as the learned.
The Lord GOD has opened My ear;
And I was not rebellious,
Nor did I turn away.
I gave My back to those who struck Me,
And My cheeks to those who plucked out the beard;
I did not hide My face from shame and spitting.
"For the Lord GOD will help Me;
Therefore, I will not be disgraced;
Therefore, I have set My face like a flint,
And I know that I will not be ashamed." (Isaiah 50:4-7)

These words speak of the Messiah roughly 800 years before He was born. Isaiah, by revelation from God, shared Christ's intimate thoughts.

Determined!

"When the days were coming to a close for Him to be taken up, He determined to journey to Jerusalem." (Luke 9:51. -*The Holman Christian Standard Bible*)

One must be determined to follow Christ at all costs. This is one of the first rules in discipleship-making. If a new believer can't commit to following the leadership structure of discipleship, that man or woman will never make a good disciple of Jesus. This must be a prerequisite for those who desire to follow Jesus!

For the Joy Set Before Him!

"Therefore we also, since we are surrounded by so great a cloud of witnesses, let us lay aside every weight, and the sin which so easily ensnares us, and let us run with endurance the race that is set before us, looking unto Jesus, the author and finisher of our faith, who for the joy that was set before Him endured the cross, despising the shame, and has sat down at the right hand of the throne of God." (Hebrews 12:1, 2)

Finally, Jesus was not only determined to follow the Father to the cross, but the Hebrew writer tells us that Jesus saw something else, He endured the cross, despising the shame of it.... and pressed in until the complete will of God had been carried through.

I believe that unless one is set on living a life that makes no reservations, with no regrets in giving all to Jesus, and will not turn back from pressing into God's full will, a man will not find pleasure in Jesus!

Dedicated to Christ!

In closing, I read a story many years ago on the Moravian Church and its dedication to serving Jesus at any cost.

This specific story said that this church would have an outreach to a nearby island, a leper colony. Only lepers lived there.

The servants of God at this Moravian church would sign up to be part of an outreach to the unsaved lepers. Of course, once you left for the island, chances were that you were not coming back!

Eventually, leprosy would get a hold of the disciple and kill him. What was interesting about this church and its disciples was that every time a disciple would die, the list would go back up at the church for new servants of God to sign up and go to the island. They couldn't wait to sign up!

Let this story go deep into your heart!

3

Leave the Fish!

And Jesus, walking by the Sea of Galilee, saw two brothers, Simon called Peter, and Andrew his brother, casting a net into the sea; for they were fishermen. Then He said to them, "Follow Me, and I will make you fishers of men." They immediately left their nets and followed Him. Going on from there, He saw two other brothers, James the son of Zebedee, and John his brother, in the boat with Zebedee their father, mending their nets. He called them, and immediately they left the boat and their father, and followed Him." (Matthew 4:18-22)

The Greatest Privilege!

Serving Jesus with full-hearted devotion can be a privilege as much as a challenge of faith. Depending on the touch of God upon your life, you will determine if it's a privilege or a challenge.

In the case of many servants of God, their fear, doubt, and lack of trust and confidence in the Lord have caused them to hold back. By holding back, I am referring not to helping or serving or giving unto the Lord what you can or what is allowed. In serving Jesus, I am speaking of total devotion in giving your life fully unto the Lord!

In following Jesus, I am speaking of a devotion that affects you first and foremost in your inner man (your heart and mind) and secondly, your outward man (ministry). People think that service unto the Lord is ministry. Doing this or doing that and running around all over town trying to be all things to all people. This is not what I am speaking of.

I've had some friends who were ministers for Jesus. They only did ministry because they liked the perks (money, fame, status, etc.) that came with the calling; they ministered fervently - until the fire burnt their man-made dream!

Without putting any rules on the subject, the call to serve Jesus begins with a life of surrender. Surrendering to the

Lord must be the first step to entering His service. When the Lord calls a man to serve Him, that is a call to die! Make no mistake here. You cannot give your life to God unless you are willing to be spent for Him.

I personally don't serve God for what others can do for me. I didn't build churches so people could come and hear me, see me, or so I could be their big brother. I didn't build bible schools or traveled on missionary trips to see the world, and I surely don't minister in Mexico because I am bored and have nothing better to do with my life!

I do what I do because He called me to do it. I can say with Paul, **"And I thank Christ Jesus our Lord who has enabled me, because He counted me faithful, putting me into the ministry, although I was formerly a blasphemer, a persecutor, and an insolent man; but I obtained mercy because I did it ignorantly in unbelief. And the grace of our Lord was exceedingly abundant, with faith and love which are in Christ Jesus. This is a faithful saying and worthy of all acceptance, that Christ Jesus came into the world to save sinners, of whom I am chief. However, for this reason I obtained mercy, that in me first Jesus Christ might show all longsuffering, as a pattern to those who are going to believe on Him for everlasting life. Now to the King eternal, immortal, invisible, to God who alone** is wise, be honor and glory forever and ever." Amen. (1 Timothy 1:12-17)

I didn't come into service to gain notoriety, fame, or status. Listen, my friends, when God called me, I was already approved in His eyes. His approval of my life is all I needed. His call was not burdensome but a genuine privilege to offer this one life He gave me.

When Jesus Sets His Eyes On You!

Every move of God begins with God, not with man. God initiates the rhythm, keeps it, and finishes it. The rhythm is His own heartbeat for the lost and His church.

As a rule to the spiritual man, it is always good to remember the Scripture in Psalm 127:1 that reads: **"Unless the Lord builds the house, those who build it labor in vain."** (RSV).

Jesus must have preeminence in everything—your life, family, business, and ministry. His presence must be first and foremost in every decision and situation.

"And Jesus, walking by the Sea of Galilee, saw two brothers, Simon called Peter, and Andrew his brother, casting a net into the sea; for they were fishermen."

While the Lord is walking by the Sea of Galilee, his eyes caught a glimpse of two people, Peter and Andrew. What were they doing? They were fishing for they were fisherman.

It seems thought-provoking that Jesus always sought people working on something practical as they lived out their lives.

When one is responsible with little, God will promote them too much. We must learn to be faithful with the little bit we know to do to catch the Lord's eye and get His attention.

I Will Make You!

As Jesus sees these fishermen, He challenges them: **"Follow Me, and I will make you fishers of men."**

Let me read out to you in its original context what this meant:

First, Jesus said, **"Follow Me."** The word carries the idea of someone coming away from something and entering something different or new. Apparently, the disciples heard Him clearly; there is no doubt about that.

As they contemplate the invitation, Jesus adds, **"And I will make you fishers of men."** What does this mean? The word make you means change. In other words, Jesus was inviting these fishermen to a life transformation! Note: The idea of **"fishers of men"** was a totally new concept to them. They needed Jesus to train them in this.

When God calls a man or a woman, he calls them to die to self; this is the first step to transformation. Here's where we get rid of our concepts and ideas. Secondly, the canvas is ready to make the necessary changes that will complement His work, idea, or purpose. Do you see this?

We don't sign up for use by God; we are first acknowledged and then invited to this life of walking with Him.

The Lord will then begin the process of change. Few understand this process, for many don't realize that what we have within us is no good to God. He must rid us of ourselves so that He may have the preeminence.

Many have felt that transformation is difficult. It's true. God will never use that old man; the old nature called the flesh. The carnal man must die before God can truly use him or her.

Immediately!

"They immediately left their nets and followed Him."
I don't know about you, but when I read the word immedi-

ately, I only understand one meaning: it means now!

As soon as the servants heard the voice of Christ, they said, "Count me in!"

To begin this life transformation, this change that Jesus spoke about, the listener would have to step into it as soon as possible. This would mark them for their entire journey with Jesus for the next three years or so!

The Lord will do the same with you and me. He will look for us first; when He finds us, He will invite us to a life of transformation. He will know who those followers are by their immediate response to His voice!

Finally, when one hears His voice to follow to whatever degree, let that individual know that provision will come from the hand of God. He is not asking you to figure your life out first, then serve Him. He is not considering your gifts, talents, and abilities. He doesn't need that. Let me remind you – He is about to change you to fit His purpose.

Many people ponder the idea of provision before giving their lives to God if God has called them. The reality is this: If God has called you to follow, then follow. If God has not asked you to follow (and only you know that), don't follow.

Remember: Only those called to follow will be held accountable whether they did or did not follow.

4

The Real You: Recognizing the Latent Power of Self & Sin!

Then Moses answered and said, "But suppose they will not believe me or listen to my voice; suppose they say, 'The LORD has not appeared to you.'"
So, the LORD said to him, "What is that in your hand?"
He said, "A rod."
And He said, "Cast it on the ground." So, he cast it on the ground, and it became a serpent, and Moses fled from it. Then the LORD said to Moses, "Reach out your hand and take it by the tail" (and he reached out his hand and

caught it, and it became a rod in his hand), "that they may believe that the LORD God of their fathers, the God of Abraham, the God of Isaac, and the God of Jacob, has appeared to you."
Furthermore, the LORD said to him, "Now put your hand in your bosom." And he put his hand in his bosom, and when he took it out, behold, his hand was leprous, like snow. And He said, "Put your hand in your bosom again." So, he put his hand in his bosom again and drew it out of his bosom, and behold, it was restored like his other flesh." (Exodus 4:1-7)

Are You Touched by God?

What an amazing journey Moses had when God touched Him! I don't believe anyone knew what God was about to do through this vessel: His name was Moses, and God had touched Him for a life of service and kingdom advancement.

As I have studied this man's life, I have come to understand more profoundly how people whom the Lord does not call to follow Him are always lagging; they don't take responsibility for God's assignment and do not make room for God to work in them.

When people can't make time for personal Bible reading,

prayer, or living a life with lost souls in mind, then I believe something is missing. I venture to say that these so-called servants are, in my opinion, not called by the Lord as they think they are!

I believe all these are signs to someone who doesn't have a call to follow or who had a call but walked away from it in their hearts and needs renewal.

It is hard to expect a believer to take steps of faith when they don't have God's faith, and why is that? God has not touched them or called them!

When the Lord touches our lives, we immediately understand the seriousness of the call.

The deposit of a call inside our hearts will also change our personal perspective of life and the world around us.

Being touched by God affects the servant in two areas: the outward life of ministry and the inward life of brokenness.

Only a few people understand this. Let me explain.

God's Ministry Credentials

"Then Moses answered and said, "But suppose they will not believe me or listen to my voice; suppose they say, 'The LORD has not appeared to you.'"

Ministry is an act of serving man unselfishly on behalf of Jesus. Since He is not present here on earth, we are the hands, feet, mouths, and eyes of Jesus here. As we move by faith in the name of Jesus, people are touched by God's Spirit that dwells richly in us.

The outward works in His name are just that, works. Many servants do this work from a pure heart and are to be acknowledged for their sacrificial service. However, we do ministry, and in many cases, it is different from what we are! I have seen people do a lot of service in the name of the church brand or church project, but not for Jesus.

Moses Gets Educated for External Ministry.

"So, the LORD said to him, "What is that in your hand?"
He said, "A rod."
And He said, "Cast it on the ground." So, he cast it on the ground, and it became a serpent, and Moses fled from it. Then the LORD said to Moses, "Reach out your hand and take it by the tail" (and he reached out his hand and caught it, and it became a rod in his hand), "that they

may believe that the LORD God of their fathers, the God of Abraham, the God of Isaac, and the God of Jacob, has appeared to you."**

A rod was the instrument that Moses owned. God asked him, **"What is that in your hand?" He said, "A rod."**

If we have faith, we believe that God will always use what we have [a rod], and we know that this is God's doing. As one man once said, We provide the natural; God delivers the supernatural.

As we advance in faith and obedience, God will vindicate His Name and perform signs and wonders through us. We should never doubt that!

If God calls us to do anything in His Name, you can rest assured that He will make it happen just as He has designed it. The call will require faithfulness and perseverance on our part—the rest God will do.

Notice how God turned the rod into a serpent in Moses's life. There was no way on earth that Moses could have converted a dead piece of wood into a serpent; this was the Lord's doing. The miracle will only happen as we move in obedience to His wishes!

Serving Jesus is a high honor and privilege but not the highest of all honors. Knowing Him is the highest of all honors.

You see, the Apostle Paul, after leading many to Christ, training workers, and building churches, still pursued something. What was it?

Listen to this: **"Brethren, I do not count myself to have apprehended, but one thing I do, forgetting those things which are behind and reaching forward to those things which are ahead, I press toward the goal for the prize of the upward call of God in Christ Jesus."** (Philippians 3:13, 14)

Moses Gets Educated in Internal Ministry.

The second part of education in ministry is what happened next in the life of Moses.

After Moses had experienced the rod turning into a serpent and then back into a rod, Moses was amazed!

Isn't it true that when we see the Lord using us somehow, we feel special and highly favored by the Lord? People around you praise you for your life, ministry, teaching, preaching gift, administration, leadership, etc. This seemed to be the case in the life of Moses.

By now, Moses feels comforted by God and is secure that God will back him up when he faces Pharaoh and God's children in Egypt.

Then things turned as God tested Moses one more time...

"Furthermore, the LORD said to him, "Now put your hand in your bosom." And he put his hand in his bosom, and when he took it out, behold, his hand was leprous, like snow. And He said, "Put your hand in your bosom again." So, he put his hand in his bosom again and drew it out of his bosom, and behold, it was restored like his other flesh."

As Moses was building up his confidence due to God's backing power, suddenly, Moses discovered that in his own bosom, in his own heart, he had leprosy that was hidden.

Moses was terrified at the sight of the ugly leprosy that was hidden deep within his own heart.

You see, what people see is not what God sees. God looks at the heart of man. He sees the rebellion, the lust, the compromise, the fears and doubts in our hearts. There is enough sin in all of us to disqualify us from doing anything for God. Are you hearing me?

Remember, leprosy is nothing more than sin - unforsaken, hidden sin! Moses discovered that in his heart he was full of it!

The Ugliness of Leprosy

1. *Leprosy Was an Inward Disease.*
Even though you saw leprosy on the outside of the body, the disease's real cause was beneath the surface. The sores and other problems were symptoms of the disease, but the cause ran more profound still. Sin is precisely the same. We are not sinners because we sin; we sin because we are sinners. The root of sin runs deep. Sin proceeds from a sinful heart.

Just like the leper would have the disease long before it even began to show, sin does its work in us well before others may ever see it. It often starts with secret sins, where only we will feel the tenderness. Then, it begins to show itself in public sin, and when we defend and justify our sin, it starts to decay and putrify, but it all starts from within.

2. *Leprosy Was a Loathsome Disease.*
It could be felt. It came with uncomfortable numbness,

aches, and unhealing wounds. Many of the scars that the leper would have resulted from the numbness the disease produced. Once the sense of pain was gone, the lepers could be cutting or burning their flesh without even knowing it. Likewise, sin stupefies us, and when our conscience is numb, it wounds.

It had a terrible odor. The aroma would drive others away, but the infected person could not escape it and, at other times, didn't even notice it. Lepers didn't even like the smell of each other, much like when two sinners get together. The sins of the other often repulse them even though their sin is just as rotten.

It could also be heard. It attacked the vocal cords, causing a raspy voice. In the same way, sin finds its most accessible escape through the tongue, which is why James warns us of its power. Even Jesus said, **"Out of the abundance of the heart, the mouth speaks."** Sin can be heard.

Leprosy could also find its way into clothing and the house's walls. Likewise, sin can manifest in how we dress and what we do with and in our homes.

In all these ways, leprosy was loathsome. It could not be kept hidden, and like leprosy, our sin will find a way out, and we will be exposed. There is no hiding the disease, especially from God.

3. Leprosy Was a Separating Disease
Leprosy put you outside of the camp for quarantine. Still, not only did it separate loved ones, like sin can destroy relationships, but it also separated the infected person from the presence of God. They were considered ceremonially unclean, which meant they could not go to the temple to worship, and the temple was where God manifested His presence. Sin does the same. It puts us at enmity with God, severing our relationship with Him and leading to our destruction.

4. The Leprous Person Could Not Cure Themselves.
During biblical times, there was no natural remedy, exercise program, diet, or topical ointments that could touch the depths of the disease. However, this lack of a cure did not mean that people were not cleansed of the disease. Miriam only had the disease for a short time on her hand, and God healed Naaman by having him wash seven times in the Jordan. What is impossible with men is possible with God.

5. Jesus Can Heal the Leper
In Matthew chapter eight, we see Jesus touch the leper. The fact that Jesus touched the leper is astounding because if anyone else had met a leper, they would have become un-

clean. Jesus, however, touches the leper, and the opposite happens; the leper becomes clean. We are sinners deserving of judgment, and God, being a just God, must punish sin. If God were to let sin go unpunished, it would mean that He would be unjust, so how could God justify sinners without himself being tainted? He did it by bearing the justice and wrath sin deserved when the Father sent the Son and died upon the cross. Those who have faith in Jesus can forgive their sins because their punishment was placed upon Christ. God will judge every sin, and His wrath will either be poured out on the sinner or upon Christ in their place. This substitution is why God can be just and the justifier of sinners.

The Real You!

Once you see the hidden leprosy in your heart, you will stop pretending who you truly are!

Too often, people get fooled by their own hearts. They think that because they come from this background, have this degree, have this job, have this type of ministry, or live by specific rules better than others, they are higher than everyone else.

If you have ever thought this of yourself, you are in for a rude awakening. God will not allow us to go very far before He brings down all our pride and arrogance.

In Proverbs 16:18, it says that **"pride comes before destruction."**

It's Time to Weep!

We see it in Peter's life when he betrayed Jesus. Peter was so sure that he wouldn't do it, but Peter never recognized the leprosy in his own heart and turned his back on Jesus! Listen to this pitiful story: **"And the Lord said, "Simon, Simon! Indeed, Satan has asked for you, that he may sift you as wheat. But I have prayed for you, that your faith should not fail; and when you have returned to Me, strengthen your brethren." But he said to Him, "Lord, I am ready to go with You, both to prison and to death." Then He said, "I tell you, Peter, the rooster shall not crow this day before you will deny three times that you know Me."** (Luke 22:31-34)

Immediately, while he was still speaking, the rooster crowed. And the Lord turned and looked at Peter. Then Peter remembered the word of the Lord, how He had said to him, "Before the rooster crows, you will deny Me three times." So, Peter went out and wept bitterly." (Luke 22:60-62)

As I close this devotion, we must humble ourselves before God daily and ask Him to search our hearts for any hidden leprosy. We should ask His Spirit to help us recognize it, quickly repent, and yield our lives thoroughly to Him!

5

Job: I Will Still Worship!

Earthly Life of Joy

There was a man in the land of Uz, whose name was Job; and that man was blameless and upright, and one who feared God and shunned evil. And seven sons and three daughters were born to him. Also, his possessions were seven thousand sheep, three thousand camels, five hundred yoke of oxen, five hundred female donkeys, and a very large household, so that this man was the greatest of all the people of the East. And his sons would go and feast in their houses, each on his appointed day, and would send and invite their three sisters to eat and drink with them. So it was, when the days of feasting had run their course, that Job would send and sanctify them, and he would rise early in the morning and offer burnt offerings according to the number of them all. For Job said, 'It may be that my sons have sinned and cursed God in their hearts.' Thus Job did regularly." (Job 1:1-5)

When I study Job's life, I can't help but notice that He was a just man. He believed in himself and attained a self-righteous status.

Here's a man who crossed all "T's" and dotted all the "I's" of life.

No one alive could come and point the finger at this man and bring reproach upon his life. No one could blame him for being religiously irresponsible; no one could point a finger and say, "You are a bad husband, the worse father, or a poor provider." Job was a man who had attained grandeur due to his pursuit of God.

Job was responsible, a man of conviction, and disciplined in all his religious practices.

In the days of Jesus, Job would have been a great Pharisee! Many of us today feel that we have attained a level of righteousness and carry about a pride that no one can see – except God!

We measure ourselves by comparing ourselves with others less fortunate than us; spiritually speaking, we feel a little higher. However, God knows the wickedness that lies deep within our selfish hearts.

I can only imagine Job's reputation. Everyone wanted to shake his hand; others wanted to attend his gatherings, yet others wanted to sit at his feet and learn from this wise servant of God.

This was Job's life as a godly servant.

From Earth's perspective, we tend to judge what we see. We don't know what we don't know. We must learn that things are not what they seem. This is why communion with the Holy Spirit is of vital importance.

Learning God's Ways!

"For My thoughts are not your thoughts,
Nor are your ways My ways," says the Lord.
"For as the heavens are higher than the earth,
So are My ways higher than your ways,

And My thoughts than your thoughts." (Isaiah 55:8)

Before continuing Job's life, let us look deep into this set of verses. Isaiah reads and says what God is saying to His people: **"My thoughts are not your thoughts."** What does this mean?

The word *thoughts* means (1) design or designs, (2) intentions, (3) plans, or (4) purposes.

Do you see how different the Lord is from us?

Often, we think that going to church without a relationship with the Holy Spirit is enough to learn God's ways, but we quickly discover that it is not like that.

When the carnal mind is in charge, we will eventually corrupt ourselves. We will fool ourselves into thinking that we are "ok," when in reality, we are, of all men, to be pitied!

One of the things that man does when he is in control of his life is to try to mimic God in his own selfish wisdom and strength. Man's designs are created by him and for himself.

It is the same way with the intentions of his own heart. His plans and purposes are somehow designed to prop him up and make him outstanding among family and peers.

In the natural, man always feels secure by his accomplishments. If a man doesn't meet his expectations, he gets discouraged; if he does, he becomes proud. **"Unless the Lord builds the house, they labor in vain who build it!"** said the Psalmist in Psalm 127:1.

In other words, if the Lord is not the One leading you and me in our everyday lives, we might experience a rude awakening - just like Job!

Spiritual Realm Realities

'Now, there was a day when the sons of God came to present themselves before the Lord, and Satan also came among them. And the Lord said to Satan, "From where do you come?" So, Satan answered the Lord and said, "From going to and fro on the earth, and from walking back and forth on it." Then the Lord said to Satan, "Have you considered My servant Job, that there is none like him on the earth, a blameless and upright man, one who fears God and shuns evil?" So, Satan answered the Lord and said, "Does Job fear God for nothing? Have You not made a hedge around him, around his household, and around all that he has on every side? You have blessed the work of his hands, and his possessions have increased in the land. But now, stretch out Your hand and touch all that he has, and he will surely curse You to Your face!" And the Lord said to Satan, "Behold, all that he has is in your power; only do not lay a hand on his person." So, Satan went out from the presence of the Lord." (Job 1:1-13)

While things are happening on Earth, they are also happening in the spiritual realm, and we must know this.

Knowing Job as a close friend, God knew that Job needed to be awakened from his self-righteousness.

Some of us need God to do thorough work deep within our hearts and transform our thinking and priorities.

So, one day, when Satan visited, the Lord asked him what he was up to. **Satan said, "From going to and fro on the earth, and from walking back and forth on it."**

Have You Considered My Servant?

This is God asking Satan if he had *considered* Job. Let us look closer at the word considered. The word **considered** in the original Hebrew is made of two words: *The first means to put, place, or set. The second word means inner man, mind, will,* *and heart.*

In essence, God was telling Satan, have you seen the heart of Job? Have you considered the way it is set?

When the Hedge is Down!

So, Satan answered the Lord and said, "Does Job fear God for nothing? Have You not made a hedge around him, around his household, and around all that he has on every side? You have blessed the work of his hands, and his possessions have increased in the land. But now, stretch out Your hand and touch all that he has, and he will surely curse You to Your face!"

Satan told God, "There are reasons why this man walks with You the way He does!"

You see church, outwardly, all the material stuff was in place. God had blessed this man with abundance: for starters, God had given him protection for himself, his family, and his goods; then he also blessed the work of his hands, which, in turn, brought great increase to his land.

Outward stuff is often recognized as God's favor on someone. But is it God's favor? Is it possible to live in sin and be blessed? Is it possible to have much materialism around you and be far away from God? Absolutely!

If materialism was the sign of a blessing upon God's people, why do drug dealers have more money than you? Why do some wicked people have more goods than you and I?

God loved this man, Job. He wasn't going to allow Job to fall by the wayside by allowing him to be eaten up with self-righteousness. God was serious about this and was about to change Job's life.

The Hour of Testing

"But now, stretch out Your hand and touch all that he has, and he will surely curse You to Your face!"

The time came for God to test His servant's heart.

Again, outwardly, everybody would be judging, but inwardly, only God knew what was in Job's heart, and God was after correcting this in his life. So, the trials began...

"Now there was a day when his sons and daughters were eating and drinking wine in their oldest brother's house; and a messenger came to Job and said, "The oxen were

plowing and the donkeys feeding beside them, when the Sabeans raided them and took them away—indeed they have killed the servants with the edge of the sword; and I alone have escaped to tell you!" While he was still speaking, another also came and said, "The fire of God fell from heaven and burned up the sheep and the servants and consumed them; and I alone have escaped to tell you!"

While he was still speaking, another also came and said, "The Chaldeans formed three bands, raided the camels and took them away, yes, and killed the servants with the edge of the sword; and I alone have escaped to tell you!" While he was still speaking, another also came and said, "Your sons and daughters were eating and drinking wine in their oldest brother's house, and suddenly a great wind came from across the wilderness and struck the four corners of the house, and it fell on the young people, and they are dead; and I alone have escaped to tell you!" Then Job arose, tore his robe, and shaved his head; and he fell to the ground and worshiped. And he said:

"Naked I came from my mother's womb,
And naked shall I return there.
The Lord gave, and the Lord has taken away;
Blessed be the name of the Lord."
In all this, Job did not sin nor charge God with wrong."
(Job 1:13-22)

Everything that had made Job famous, that gave him significance and status among his countrymen, all of it disappeared in a day!

Considered a Second Time!

"Again, there was a day when the sons of God came to present themselves before the Lord, and Satan came also among them to present himself before the Lord. And the Lord said to Satan, "From where do you come?"
Satan answered the Lord and said, "From going to and fro on the earth, and from walking back and forth on it."
Then the Lord said to Satan, "Have you considered My servant Job, that there is none like him on the earth, a blameless and upright man, one who fears God and shuns evil? And still he holds fast to his integrity, although you incited Me against him, to destroy him without cause."
So, Satan answered the Lord and said, "Skin for skin! Yes, all that a man has he will give for his life. But stretch out Your hand now, and touch his bone and his flesh, and he will surely curse You to Your face!"
And the Lord said to Satan, "Behold, he is in your hand, but spare his life."
So, Satan went out from the presence of the Lord and struck Job with painful boils from the sole of his foot to the crown of his head. And he took for himself a potsherd

with which to scrape himself while he sat in the midst of the ashes.
Then his wife said to him, "Do you still hold fast to your integrity? Curse God and die!"
But he said to her, "You speak as one of the foolish women speaks. Shall we indeed accept good from God, and shall we not accept adversity?" In all this, Job did not sin with his lips." (Job 2:1-10).

The Lord was testing Job's heart and health to a great degree—have you ever been there in your own walk?

You see, God is more interested in you than material things. People in our nation have become worshipers of created things and have neglected the Creator!

Made in His Image!

As we walk with God, the Holy Spirit will bring to the forefront anything and everything that is not of God. He will expose it to you so you may clear it from your life. He will work deep in the heart and mind of man to purify him or her for His good pleasure.

Is God against material stuff? I don't believe He is. I believe God is against anything that tries to conform us to an image different from His. There are things that have possessed us and robbed us of His image. I believe Job was being tested deeply in His character.

Job Worshipped Despite All the Pain.

Many wonder when my trial will end. When will all this adversity come to a stop? You know you have asked yourself that many times. Let me tell you...until you get the lesson! Until you come to where God speaks and reveals why things are going on this way or in our lives. Then and only then, things subside.

Job came to a place where he was being squeezed like a honeycomb and finally surrendered his heart and said: **"Though He slay me, yet will I trust Him."** (Job 13:15)

We look at ourselves and make conclusions about ourselves; people look at our lives and make conclusions about our lives, but God sees us the way it is! He sets all things in motion around us. Can you see this? Can you perceive the Holy Spirit speaking?

In closing, let me encourage your heart with these words: **"Abide in Me, and I in you. As the branch cannot bear fruit of itself unless it abides in the vine, neither can** you unless you abide in Me. "I am the vine; you are the branches. He who abides in Me, and I in him, bears much fruit; for without Me you can do nothing." (John 15:4, 5)

6

The True Friends of God!

"This is My commandment, that you love one another as I have loved you. Greater love has no one than this than to lay down one's life for his friends. You are My friends if you do whatever I command you. No longer do I call you servants, for a servant does not know what his master is doing; but I have called you friends, for all things that I heard from My Father I have made known to you. You did not choose Me, but I chose you and appointed you that you should go and bear fruit and that your fruit should remain ..." (John 15:12-16)

As Christ began to teach His servants about love and what it meant to love God's way, He spoke to them at a very different level. He defined what it meant to love by teaching them that no greater love has any man than to lay down his life for his friends.

He added, **"You are my friends if you do whatever I command you."** Ponder this for a while. Jesus defines true friendship with the Father as loving God so that one will obey Him, even unto death! Do you understand this?

For the most part, Jesus had been teaching the disciples about God's kingdom and what God had in store for all who followed Him. The prophecies and the promises were all given as signs of God's presence and assurance in their lives. Yet, there appeared to be a disconnection between man and God.

The disciples had an attitude of servanthood. They wanted to please Jesus in every way possible. They were ready to act for Him; you will see that all through the New Testament. They served Him and did signs and wonders along with Him. They learned many things concerning the kingdom of God, but not all.

Serving Jesus is only the beginning of love, but intimately knowing Jesus is something different. To know the Lord is the beginning of wisdom. Knowing the Lord intimately is the secret power most believers lack in the church today.

You see, one can serve God or at least help in the "name of Jesus," if you will. This is what we call servants.

Many believers aspire to this kind of religious practice. Their spiritual experience is mainly outward and selfish. They associate servanthood with friendship, but it is not the same thing.

Anyone can come and offer to be a servant, but no one can come to Jesus and say, "I want to be your friend because I like you." Friends are invited into God's circle of friends. You only come by invitation.

No Longer Do I Call You Servants!

Then it happened that Jesus said, "No longer do I call you servants, for a servant does not know what his master is doing; but I have called you friends, for all things that I heard My Father I have made known to you." (John 15:15)

Jesus allows His disciples to come closer to His heart by making them friends. This was the door to revelation for them. From this point on, the disciples and friends of Jesus would begin to hear a little more of the insight into the Father's heart through Jesus.

What Jesus was doing was preparing them for the day when the Holy Spirit would come and take them to a whole new level of wisdom and revelation.

One thing to note here is that as human beings in our flesh, we are limited in what we can do for Jesus. We may help and serve simply because it is convenient, or we have time. Yet, the friends of God are not like this. They hear God and act according to the divine orders given. It has nothing to do with any external condition.

Secrets Reserved, But for Who?

"I still have many things to say to you, but you cannot bear them now. However, when He, the Spirit of truth, has come, He will guide you into all truth; for He will not speak on His own authority, but whatever He hears He will speak; and He will tell you things to come. He will glorify Me, for He will take of what is Mine and declare it to you. All things that the Father has are Mine. Therefore, I said that He will take of Mine and declare it to you." (John 16:12-16)

There is a reason the Lord only goes so far in sharing His heart with His servants; John 16:12 tells us exactly why. Jesus told them about the Holy Spirit, whom He would send in His stead, **"I still have many things to say to you, but you cannot bear them now."**

The word *bear* has a lot of depth to it. Let me share. The word *bear* in Greek means several things: *1) It means to lift or exalt. 2) It means to carry. 3) It also means to lift a veil. 4) It means to hold in one's hands. 5) It means to touch or embrace. 6) It means to consider and weigh. 7) It means to produce, yield, of land.*

So, apparently, Jesus is making a huge statement here. He is basically saying, "There are lots of things I will show you, but I cannot do it now. You are not at that place yet! You will not grasp its eternal message—but the time will come."

As the Spirit Comes!

But as it is written:
"Eye has not seen, nor ear heard,
Nor have entered into the heart of man
The things which God has prepared for those who love Him."
But God has revealed them to us through His Spirit. For

the Spirit searches all things, yes, the deep things of God. For what man knows the things of a man except the spirit of the man which is in him? Even so no one knows the things of God except the Spirit of God. Now we have received, not the spirit of the world, but the Spirit who is from God, that we might know the things that have been freely given to us by God." (1 Corinthians 2:9-12)

As the Spirit of God begins to take His role in us, He will begin to reveal to you and me the things concerning God, His purpose, and His plan for you. God is the one who makes you bear these revelations. He is the One who illuminates us with truth.

Chosen for Producing Fruit!

"You did not choose Me, but I chose you and appointed you that you should go and bear fruit and that your fruit should remain..." (John 15:16)

In our pursuit of God, almost always, the Lord will lead us into His harvest. Yes, He will heal, deliver, and anoint you, but this is not only for you. You are called to take what Jesus has shown you into the world primarily, not so much the church.

Our goal as His servants is to press in until we get His attention and become His friends. It is here that the high calling of God in Christ Jesus begins and ends. It is at this place that the heavens are open to you and me, for the Lord knows that He can trust us with divine revelation to hear and act.

7

Stay Focused With God's Plan!

In my desire to communicate how the life of Jesus must be our priority above all things, I want you to turn in your Bible to the book of Matthew chapter 3 and focus on how a touch from God will impact us:

"Then Jesus came from Galilee to John at the Jordan to be baptized by him. And John tried to prevent Him, saying, "I need to be baptized by You, and are You coming to me?" But Jesus answered and said to him, "Permit it to be so now, for thus it is fitting for us to fulfill all righteousness." Then he allowed Him. When He had been baptized, Jesus came up immediately from the water; behold, the heavens were opened to Him, and He saw the Spirit of God descending like a dove and alighting upon Him. And suddenly a voice came from heaven, saying, "This is My beloved Son, in whom I am well pleased." (Matthew 3:13-17)**

In our walk with God, one thing is sure - to the degree that God has touched us is to the degree that we will make God-directed decisions. The less intense our commitment, the more compromising our lives will be.

One may wonder why "so and so" is not as committed or compare one's spiritual growth with somebody else. In many instances, people even question why one's ministry is more extensive or more influential than someone else's.

Do these things matter? Should we be concerned about this or that? Many do, especially the immature. They concern themselves with things that are truly not important to them.

As we begin to embrace our life with God and, as John the Baptist said, the "More of Him and less of Me" lifestyle, we will learn that some things are not as important as we think. In fact, we must learn to be God-pleasers and not man-pleasers.

What Kind of Baptism Did You Receive?

"And it happened, while Apollos was at Corinth, that Paul, having passed through the upper regions, came to Ephesus. And finding some disciples he said to them, "Did you receive the Holy Spirit when you believed?"
So they said to him, "We have not so much as heard whether there is a Holy Spirit."
And he said to them, "Into what then were you baptized?"
So they said, "Into John's baptism."
Then Paul said, "John indeed baptized with a baptism of repentance, saying to the people that they should believe on Him who would come after him, that is, on Christ Jesus."
When they heard this, they were baptized in the name of the Lord Jesus. And when Paul had laid hands on them, the Holy Spirit came upon them, and they spoke with tongues and prophesied. Now the men were about twelve in all." (Acts 19:1-7)

Here's an example where some of the early disciples went to see John the Baptist baptizing people in the River Jordan and got themselves into the water with a baptism of repentance.

They pledge allegiance to follow the teachings of Christ at this point. In Bible times, anyone baptized into a "name" meant that they would publicly affirm that they followed that person's teachings.

But this type of baptism was a ritual and an external act of obedience.

Paul's Baptism

"Do you not know that all of us who have been baptized into Christ Jesus were baptized into his death? We were buried therefore with him by baptism into death, in order that, just as Christ was raised from the dead by the glory of the Father, we too might walk in newness of life." (Romans 6:3, 4)

The Scripture in the book of Romans teaches that those who have been baptized into Christ Jesus were baptized into his death. We were buried and then resurrected by the glory of the Father so that we might walk in the newness of life! Think about this.

The word *baptized* in Greek means, "βάπτω, "to dip in or under" "to dye," used in Josephus only in this sense, "dyed material," the sense of "to immerse" (trans.) from the time of Hippocrates, in Plato and esp. in later writers, "to sink the ship."

It is essential to know the degree of this baptism you experienced when Christ touched your life and entered your heart. Many take water baptisms as an act of obedience but with no power. In other words, the person getting baptized has not made Jesus the Lord of their hearts. They are only merely carrying out a ritual, which, without conversion, you are only getting wet!

All I can say is that baptism is a serious matter, for it brings you under the lordship of Christ and under the direction of the Anointing, the Holy Spirit!

Christ Our Pattern.

"Then Jesus was led up by the Spirit..." (Matthew 4:1)

The Spirit of God is now leading Jesus. This is one of the first characteristics of a person truly walking under the anointing, under the Holy Spirit's direction.

Our lives must become more and more sensitive to the voice of God. You and I know that we are bombarded with many voices. Most of the external voices and sounds we hear have nothing to do with us or the Holy Spirit's direction in our lives. It may have significance for someone else but not for you. We are called to walk out the direction God has tailored for us.

As we learn God's heart personally, we will be able to set goals and make a difference in our lives and the lives of others.

"...into the wilderness to be tempted by the devil."

Jesus encounters the devil.

If you notice, a God-ordained life will be a life led by God. The Lord brings us into situations that will be used to prove our lives. Our character, emotions, obedience, resolve [commitment] – all of these will be tested in the wilderness by the enemy.

You don't rebuke the devil when you know God has sent him your way to test you. You only rebuke him after you see what God's intentions are. Once you know that the devil has come to test your commitment and you don't quit but pass the test, you rebuke him out of your life, but not before learning God's intention.

Think of this: When using a hammer and nailing wood, if you miss the nail and hit your hand, you feel the pain; you scream, but you don't throw the hammer away initially. You keep hammering until you are finished. Why don't you throw it away? Because it is helpful to you. Same thing with the devil.

One thing to notice is that as we obey the Holy Spirit, we are spiritually speaking, piercing the darkness; this will bring repercussions. The enemy does push back when we intend to demolish darkness. Have you found that to be true?

Test #1

"When the tempter came to Him, he said, "If You are the Son of God, command that these stones become bread." But He answered and said, "It is written, 'Man shall not live by bread alone, but by every word that proceeds from the mouth of God.'" (Matthew 4:3-5)

His first test came by way of testing his flesh. Jesus had been on a fast and was weak and very hungry.

If you haven't figured it out yet, the flesh, that entity that lives in us, will manifest itself and challenge the will of God for our lives if not kept in check. We must continually fellowship with the Spirit of God to overcome these vicious usurping thoughts.

We must also learn to walk in God's design, sphere, purpose, and timing.

Test #2

**"Then the devil took Him up into the holy city, set Him on the pinnacle of the temple, and said to Him, "If You are the Son of God, throw Yourself down. For it is written:
'He shall give His angels charge over you,'
and,
'In their hands they shall bear you up,
Lest you dash your foot against a stone.' "
Jesus said to him, "It is written again, 'You shall not tempt the Lord your God.'"** (Matthew 4:5-7)

One of the most significant tests for all of us who trust Christ is provision. For some reason, we can talk and write about His provision, shout about His provision, and sing about His provision, but when it comes to offering our time, money, and lives, we fail the test.

Don't say that you love Him and that He is your provider if you can't trust Him with your life and future, your giving of the tithes and offerings, and even your commitment to service because you don't have time for Him.

Test #3

Finally, Jesus encountered His most significant test when the

devil took him to a mountain, listen: **"Again, the devil took Him up on an exceedingly high mountain, and showed Him all the kingdoms of the world and their glory. And he said to Him, "All these things I will give You if You will fall down and worship me."**
Then Jesus said to him, "Away with you, Satan! For it is written, 'You shall worship the Lord your God, and Him only you shall serve.' "
Then the devil left Him, and behold, angels came and ministered to Him." (Matthew 4:8-11).

Apparently, the devil had been holding off on this test. When the devil found out that Jesus was not giving in to the last two tests, he went for the big one – the bowing and worshiping to receive, in exchange for the kingdoms of the world. Remember, Jesus came with the end to restore those kingdoms back to the Father.

The devil was trying to make it easy on Jesus by saying, "You don't have to die on a cross like a criminal Jesus. We can bypass all that. All you have to do is fall down and worship me, and I will give you what you came to die for! It's an opportunity of a lifetime Jesus!"

This test was a big one since it involved his own life. Everything was on the line with this test—his life, humanity, future governments—and there was lots to think about.

Despite all that was on the line, Jesus kept his focus and said, **"You shall worship the Lord your God, and Him only you shall serve!"** Angels then ministered to Jesus.

Two Things to Know about Our Focus

First, you must know that the enemy constantly challenges us to lose our focus, confidence, faith, and future.

Secondly, the Father allows these tests [by using the devil] to come our way so that we are exercised in our faith. Nothing comes our way unless the Lord permits this to happen to you.

"Consider it wholly joyful, my brethren, whenever you are enveloped in or encounter trials of any sort or fall into various temptations. Be assured and understand that the trial and proving of your faith bring out endurance and steadfastness and patience. But let endurance and steadfastness and patience have full play and do a thorough work, so that you may be [people] perfectly and fully developed [with no defects], lacking in nothing." (James 1:2-4 *Amplified Version*)

8

Face to Face!

"All the people saw the pillar of cloud standing at the tabernacle door, and all the people rose and worshiped, each man in his tent door. So, the Lord spoke to Moses face to face, as a man speaks to his friend." (Exodus 33:10-11)

When reading this small portion of Scripture and studying the events that brought us to this place in Exodus, we must realize that God wants to have fellowship with His people. The nearer, the better!

Some don't know this. Some don't realize that God's intentions have to do with the restoration of fellowship and then intimacy with Him!

In our study of More of Jesus...Less of Me! I want to take you behind the heart of God and show you why Moses was a different man in his generation. After all, it is not an everyday occurrence that you see a man lead two and a half million Hebrew children out of Egyptian bondage.

If your initial experience with God has been face-to-face, I believe the trend to meet Him in this fashion becomes the norm throughout your life. You don't see God's face once and forget about it – ever! The experience will be so embedded in your spirit that it will follow you for the rest of your life here on earth.

So, if you have never seen God face to face, ask Him to reveal Himself in this way. When He appears to you, I guarantee your life will be turned upside down. Everything about you: your thinking, emotions, ambitions, desires, plans, all of it- will be transformed to align with His!

The Early Life of Moses

"And a man of the house of Levi went and took as wife a daughter of Levi. So the woman conceived and bore a son. And when she saw that he was a beautiful child, she hid him three months. But when she could no longer hide him, she took an ark of bulrushes for him, daubed it with asphalt and pitch, put the child in it, and laid it in the reeds by the river's bank." (Exodus 2:1-3)

"Now it came to pass in those days, when Moses was grown, that he went out to his brethren and looked at their burdens. And he saw an Egyptian beating a Hebrew, one of his brethren. So he looked this way and that way, and when he saw no one, he killed the Egyptian and hid him in the sand." (Exodus 2:11, 12)

Moses was born for God's purpose, and you and I have been born for God's purpose. We might think we know what we are doing or where we are going, but so does God, and we are usually not moving in the same direction.

As he grew, the man Moses felt in his heart the need to help the Hebrew children. It was embedded in His nature to be a deliverer, but it had to be done in God's way and in His time.

Every time we move in the flesh, we will miss the mark. We will waste energy, time, and money and end up hurting people.

For forty years, Moses served Pharaoh until he killed an Egyptian, thinking he was in the perfect will of God. So, he fled to the land of Midian and hid in a desert for another forty years.

"Then Moses was content to live with the man, and he gave Zipporah his daughter to Moses." (Exodus 2:21)

The word content means in the Hebrew language to be pleased.

There comes a time in our lives when we are so discouraged by our present condition that we park. We so easily get pleased with our present way of living that we forget what God had intended for us.

We quiet the passion, the zeal, the vision, the purpose, and the plan ever to be used by the Lord. How easy is this to do? It is so easy that even Moses, with all he had experienced up to date, fell into a state of ease.

I venture to say that nothing will get us out of a state of ease until we have a fresh, face-to-face encounter with God.

A Face-to-Face Encounter!

"Now Moses was tending the flock of Jethro his father-in-law, the priest of Midian. And he led the flock to the back

of the desert, and came to Horeb, the mountain of God. And the Angel of the Lord appeared to him in a flame of fire from the midst of a bush. So he looked, and behold, the bush was burning with fire, but the bush was not consumed. Then Moses said, "I will now turn aside and see this great sight, why the bush does not burn."
So when the Lord saw that he turned aside to look, God called to him from the midst of the bush and said, "Moses, Moses!"
And he said, "Here I am."
Then He said, "Do not draw near this place. Take your sandals off your feet, for the place where you stand is holy ground." Moreover He said, "I am the God of your father—the God of Abraham, the God of Isaac, and the God of Jacob." And Moses hid his face, for he was afraid to look upon God." (Exodus 3:1-6)

Defining a Face-to-Face Lifestyle

Supernatural Encounter

When it comes to a divine call, we must first understand that a divine call is what it is - a divine call brought about by a supernatural encounter with God. It is almost as if God pulls back a curtain and allows the servant of God to see beyond the natural and is overtaken by what I call a face-to-face encounter.

The Hearing of His Voice.

After that encounter, God's servant will be overtaken by a divine voice, a heavenly voice that he or she understands it to be God. In the inner man, it registers clearly. It usually causes unsettledness in the natural, but the deep subtle peace of God hovers over the natural man. Have you even heard His voice this way?

The Invitation to Walk in Alignment With God.

This event is portrait here in the life of Moses by the taking off the sandals. This meant that Moses must take off his rights. Yes, the rights that we feel we have as an individual and place our life and everything we desire at the feet of Jesus and wait upon His mercy. This can only be done by revelation, not by willful choice alone. Many have tried to follow God in their own strength and do things according to their understanding; however, God has a divine plan laid out for the servant who takes off his sandals [rights].

The Pursuit of God's Wishes.

Finally, we are left with nothing more and nothing less than a choice to follow God's wishes. His wishes are the desires of His heart and mind. Before anyone can hear His heart and mind, one must be surrendered. The servant of God must have taken off his sandals and be willing to stand in God's presence until God commissions Him for the work.

People pray to the Lord and always talk to Him, so they claim; however, what happened to Moses was no ordinary prayer time. This was an encounter, a face-to-face encounter with the living God!

The Scripture says that Moses couldn't look upon the Lord until He followed through with God's request. I believe that it will be the same way with us.

Many of us have done great works for Jesus, but doing something for Him after encountering Him face-to-face is an altogether different calling.

The Work!

Definition of the Work.

"Now in the church that was at Antioch there were certain prophets and teachers: Barnabas, Simeon who was called Niger, Lucius of Cyrene, Manaen who had been brought up with Herod the tetrarch, and Saul. As they ministered to the Lord and fasted, the Holy Spirit said,

"Now separate to Me Barnabas and Saul for the work to which I have called them." Then, having fasted and prayed, and laid hands on them, they sent them away." (Acts 13:1-3)

The work that I am speaking of, is a specific call to a specific task. It's a focused approach to one of God's wishes. A face-to-face encounter with God will bring about such a task.

The Apostle Paul had already traveled to various provinces, planted churches, discipled God's servants, and had become one of the outstanding leaders among the apostles. Nevertheless, God was not finished with his servant Paul. God had other things lined up for him just as he has many things lined up for you and me.

The work is a specific touch of God for a specific work and for a specific season in our lives.

When I speak in this book about the title More of Jesus…and Less of Me! I am speaking to a group of servants who understand the heart of God regarding His invitation to them.

The invitation evolves around the idea of coming and walking in divine order for the purpose of accomplishing God's wishes; this is the highest calling.

If a man allows for God to align him by being submissive to the Spirit's leadership, this man, without doubt, will find himself doing the work!

9

Leaning!

"By faith Jacob, when he was dying, blessed each of the sons of Joseph, and worshiped, leaning on the top of his staff." (Hebrews 11:21)

A Life Filled with Challenges!

Before unfolding this truth, I want to take time to say that, at the end of his life, Jacob had experienced many obstacles. Some obstacles were inward, and some were outward. Nevertheless, Jacob was tested severely in his lifetime.

The picture shown to us at the end of his life as he began blessing Joseph's children, was that of leaning upon a staff in worship.

To some, a staff may not mean as much as it did to Jacob. This staff made all the difference in his life. A staff will mean a lot to us once God touches us, too.

Jacob's Beginnings

"This is the genealogy of Isaac, Abraham's son. Abraham begot Isaac. Isaac was forty years old when he took Rebekah as wife, the daughter of Bethuel the Syrian of Padan Aram, the sister of Laban the Syrian. Now Isaac pleaded with the LORD for his wife, because she was barren; and the LORD granted his plea, and Rebekah his wife conceived. But the children struggled together within her; and she said, "If all is well, why am I like this?" So she went to inquire of the LORD.
And the LORD said to her:
"Two nations are in your womb,
Two peoples shall be separated from your body;
One people shall be stronger than the other,
And the older shall serve the younger."

So when her days were fulfilled for her to give birth, indeed there were twins in her womb. And the first came out red. He was like a hairy garment all over; so they called his name Esau. Afterward his brother came out, and his hand took hold of Esau's heel; so his name was called Jacob. Isaac was sixty years old when she bore them.

So the boys grew. And Esau was a skillful hunter, a man of the field; but Jacob was a mild man, dwelling in tents. And Isaac loved Esau because he ate of his game, but Rebekah loved Jacob.

Now Jacob cooked a stew; and Esau came in from the field, and he was weary. And Esau said to Jacob, "Please feed me with that same red stew, for I am weary." Therefore his name was called Edom.

But Jacob said, "Sell me your birthright as of this day."
And Esau said, "Look, I am about to die; so what is this birthright to me?"
Then Jacob said, "Swear to me as of this day."

So he swore to him, and sold his birthright to Jacob. And Jacob gave Esau bread and stew of lentils; then he ate and drank, arose, and went his way. Thus Esau despised his birthright." (Genesis 25:19-34)

Characteristics of the Old Nature, the Flesh!

As we study Jacob's life, we will learn that he was truly a man who lived for himself—yes, a man who didn't care about anyone but himself. Have you met people like this? I'm sure you have.

The simple fact that he was Isaac's son didn't make him holy or perfect. Trying to hide behind the veil of family tradition or religious status would be quickly exposed.

In Luke 6:41, the Scripture says, **"For a good tree does not bear bad fruit, nor does a bad tree bear good fruit. For every tree is known by its own fruit."** (Luke 6:43, 44)

In considering and evaluating your life over the last few years, what kind of fruit have you produced?

For us who have given our lives to Jesus, we must understand a few things:

    a. From a lost sinner, you get into Christ (salvation) this is the beginning of your life in God.

    b. Secondly, we get the indwelling of the Spirit. This is the realization that God lives in you and your life is for His purposes. (2 Corinthians 5:15)

    c. Thirdly, the receiving of the infilling of the Spirit involves inviting God to fill you with His Spirit (spiritual gifts, power, and authority are gained here).

    d. Then, fourthly, comes the anointing. This is a time when God anoints your life for His service. It's a touch of God to serve Him.

    e. The ministry of fire (consecration) speaks of a life given wholly to Jesus and consecrated for God alone.

Hopefully, these steps will help us realize how serious this study will be and how it will impact us.

Breaking of Self! (Genesis 32:22-32)

Jacob was marked by God while living his life. He wasn't just anybody; there was a divine call upon his life. Another thing to notice about someone marked by God is how God directs their lives.

For some reason, people whom God marks walk down a different path. It's the path that few want to take.

Leaning!

Now, people who walk this path do understand that God has unfinished business with them. God is molding the man or the woman to His likeness and for His use.

"And he arose that night and took his two wives, his two female servants, and his eleven sons, and crossed over the ford of Jabbok. He took them, sent them over the brook, and sent over what he had. Then Jacob was left alone; and a Man wrestled with him until the breaking of day. Now when He saw that He did not prevail against him, He touched the socket of his hip; and the socket of Jacob's hip was out of joint as He wrestled with him. And He said, "Let Me go, for the day breaks."
But he said, "I will not let You go unless You bless me!"
So He said to him, "What is your name?"
He said, "Jacob."
And He said, "Your name shall no longer be called Jacob, but Israel; for you have struggled with God and with men, and have prevailed."
Then Jacob asked, saying, "Tell me Your name, I pray."
And He said, "Why is it that you ask about My name?"
And He blessed him there.
So Jacob called the name of the place Peniel: "For I have seen God face to face, and my life is preserved." Just as he crossed over Penuel the sun rose on him, and he limped on his hip. Therefore to this day the children of

Israel do not eat the muscle that shrank, which is on the hip socket, because He touched the socket of Jacob's hip in the muscle that shrank." (Genesis 32:22-34)

Notice how Jacob was left alone; this is a characteristic of a man about to learn God's ways. God will take this man through the mill and test his resolve, calling, emotions, will, etc. Everything that this man thinks he will be tested severely – such as Jacob.

Fighting with an Angel is a type of us fighting with God. It tests our deepest fears, sins, ideas, ambitions, plans, and everything we hold sacred. God will test all these and will win. He won't stop until He breaks us.

The Blessing of a Limp!

The Scripture says that the Lord blessed Jacob after fighting with the Angel. The blessing came in the form of a dislocation. Jacob was no longer to run; He could no longer "show off!" Jacob could no longer get away with much of what He used to before He was broken.

A life of brokenness is a life that says, *"I no longer want what I want; I want what God has in store for me!"*

Characteristics of a Transformed Life: A Life Fully Dependent Upon God.

- Led by the Holy Spirit – A life led by God's wishes, no matter what it is!
- Walk in Humility – God is always first.

- Walk in Surrender & Yieldedness – I don't want to do anything that comes from me.

- Walk in Obedience—In a life of obedience, nothing is impossible if God tells me to do it!

- Live a Life of Worship – This has to do with a heart that yearns for the presence of God all day long, forever and ever. **"As a deer pant for the water brook, so my soul pants for thee."** (Psalm 42:1)

10

"Mold Me Until It Seems Good to You, Oh God!"

The word which came to Jeremiah from the LORD, saying: "Arise and go down to the potter's house, and there I will cause you to hear My words." Then I went down to the potter's house, and there he was, making something at the wheel. And the vessel that he made of clay was marred in the hand of the potter; so he made it again into another vessel, as it seemed good to the potter to make. Then the word of the LORD came to me, saying: "O house of Israel, can I not do with you as this potter?" says the LORD. "Look, as the clay is in the potter's hand, so are you in My hand, O house of Israel!" (Jeremiah 18:1-6)

In closing my manuscript on brokenness and the deep desire to please God in all things, I thought about how the Lord teaches us obedience through His Word and makes it a point to illustrate the inner workings of His Spirit deep in our hearts.

When living for the Lord, we must never forget one thing: He didn't just die to save us; He also died to use us as His mouth, ears, hands, and feet. We are genuinely His representatives here on earth. We are being molded and shaped into His likeness daily.

Every test, trial, and temptation is a simple lesson that puts us under probation of the Holy Spirit as He shapes us into Christlikeness!

Obedience in the Smallest Things!

It was just another typical day in the life of Jeremiah the Prophet when God called him and told him, "Arise and go down to the potter's house, and there I will cause you to hear My words."

I'm amazed at the thought of this set of instructions God gave Jeremiah. God didn't come and talk to him at his own house; the Lord needed Jeremiah to take some steps outside his environment and visit the potter's home, for this would be where God would speak to Him.

It is crucial to obey the Lord, even in the most minor things! You see, it is moving out in obedience to the slightest gestures of God that connects us with divine appointments.

One evening in prayer, I remember the Lord speaking to me about attending a Prophetic Conference in Houston, Texas. I thought to myself, "What for? What will I learn, or what will another prophet say?" My attitude was not one of expectation for this event; honestly, I didn't want to attend, and God knew it.

The Lord proceeded to hunt me down and told me that a sign that He desired me to be there was that He would speak to me in a very prophetic way at the first meeting on the opening night. So, I felt the Lord wanted me to go, so I bought my plane and conference tickets.

When I arrived at the conference hall, I signed up and was ready for my prophetic encounter. The meeting started, and the worship was incredible; however, I didn't experience any touch of God. The speaker came and shared a powerful Word and ministered to the people, for which I worked up some courage and went to the front for prayer. Perhaps this was the sign that God had told me about. As I went forward for prayer, nothing spectacular happened either. Finally, the host started to pray for the dismissal of the meeting, saying, we will see you guys in the morning session at 9 am. Goodnight.

As I was getting my Bible from my chair, I felt disheartened that I had not had an experience as promised by the Lord. I was heartbroken! As I headed to the back tables where the books and CDs were, an elderly sister in the Lord, probably in her 90s, caught up to me and said, I have been watching you all through the service, and the Lord wants you to know.... She proceeded to read my mail and prophesy of my future in God. It was so powerful, and the words of the Lord through her servant were so piercing that I spent the next 30 days having prophetic visions and dreams from the Lord.

I share this story because the Lord may want to do deep work in your life and may want you to take a small step of faith so He can get the ball rolling. But if we ignore His counsel and don't obey, we will miss all God has for this season.

Jeremiah wouldn't miss what God had, so he went to the potter's house!

At the Potter's House!

As Jeremiah came to the potter's house, the potter was working away. As per the potter, it was another day at the office; but for Jeremiah, the message was one of eternal proportions.

We will always experience God from the place of spiritual maturity that we find ourselves. We will feel, hear, see, sense, smell, and understand God, based on our spiritual posture in Him.

Jeremiah came to hear God and see God work His mysteries. Jeremiah was about to get front seats to God's eternal show.

What Is God Making?

"...and there he was, making something..."

I don't know about you, but it doesn't seem like much when God begins working in our lives. We don't know what He wants to do with us; thus, Jeremiah said, **"...and there he was, making something."**

When dealing with God and the work of His hands, things usually look like this: There is no shape, no labels, no promises, no guarantees, just God working away in us. This can be very chaotic or confusing at times!

Mold Me Until It Seems Good to You, Oh God! As Jeremiah took a closer look, he noticed that the potter had a marred clay vessel in his hands. What does it mean that it was marred? The word *marred* means *to go to ruin*. What the potter was working on was made of clay; this vessel in his hand was ruined, corrupt, and useless.

Another Vessel!

"...so, he made it again into another vessel..."

Jeremiah captured the full picture. The potter understood that the clay vessel was ruined, so he made it again into another vessel.

This prophet of God was shown God's mind by observing the potter at work on his wheel. Jeremiah saw a marred clay vessel and how the potter made a new one. What distinguished the second vessel? The answer is: **"It seemed good to the potter!"**

God will appreciate our work in the flesh, but He will hold in high esteem the work done in His Name. The tasks that God orders from His priorities list reflect what is in His heart. I believe God will bless our sacrificial efforts, but why not engage in what God is already blessing instead?

Let us examine the phrase **"It seemed good** [to the potter]**."** This combination of words signifies the following: *to be smooth, straight, or correct.* It also refers to *an eye.*

The potter continued shaping the clay vessel until it was smooth, straight, and true. His eye assessed this. This mirrors what God does with His people, whom He selects to fulfill His purposes.

The Word of the Lord is Confirmed!

"Look, as the clay is in the potter's hand, so are you in My hand, O house of Israel!"

God intended to reveal His thoughts and emotions to His prophet regarding His love for His people. He allowed Jeremiah to comprehend what God was trying to accomplish with Israel.

It is also clear that we, the body of Christ, share the same predicament: God is working within us to bring us to a place where we can be of greater service to Him!

Time for You To Mold Me God!

Attitude of the Mind - I have heard church leaders say that sometimes people "don't get it!" This indicates that the leader perceives situations from one perspective, while the follower (church member) views them from another. The first thing to consider here is that the pastor or leader operates on a different (spiritual) level, and the follower, as you can imagine, is on a lesser (spiritual) level.

All servants of the Lord should embody a mindset of humility rather than pride and adopt a learner's heart instead of an arrogant attitude. Indeed, this mindset must transform into that of a humble servant who seeks to learn from God.

Attitude of the Heart – The heart of a servant who longs to please God must always be open, sensitive, and attentive to God's heart. Knowing how the Lord feels regarding an issue is something valuable to gain; understanding why the Lord Jesus would weep over a matter is also beneficial. Listen to God's heart by leaning upon it as you pray.

Quick Obedience—This issue with obedience must be understood. When God asks us to do something for Him, we can't drag our feet, be double-minded, or be lax about acting. When God says something to us, it usually means now, not tomorrow, the next day, or the next!

Whatever the cost! – Life can be expensive, so what will we do when God comes knocking, asking, "Give me your whole life?" This presents a significant challenge for anyone. However, the servant who wishes to please God will always need to strive for His will to be fulfilled within them. Serving Jesus is indeed costly, and by costly, I mean having the willingness and attitude to consider everything you cherish as "precious" and view it as a loss!   Nothing less than this type of sacrifice will do.

Worship: You are Worthy of It All! – The servant of Jesus who understands God's heart and His purposes will live a worship life. He or she will see their general life as a life of offering unto the Lord. Daily living is just another set of hours that they may worship the King of Glory with their whole being. Whether with talents, skills, money, songs, or day-to-day witnessing, God's faithful servant will always see it as worship unto Jesus!

Conclusion: "I Don't Want to be Anything Big!"

"You, therefore, must endure hardship as a good soldier of Jesus Christ. No one engaged in warfare entangles himself with the affairs of this life, that he may please him who enlisted him as a soldier." (2 Timothy 2:3, 4)

In my journey with God, I have learned a few things that have better prepared me to walk with passion and commitment unto Him. Living the life God requires is nothing short of challenging.

At times, the challenge has more to do with me than it has to do with anything external that comes my way. For example, in pleasing God, I would love to live a life of obedience and free from self, temptation, and sin. Who doesn't?

For someone who loves God, nothing is more disheartening than to break His heart by my constant disobedience, my constant rebellion or passive rebellion, my increased selfish passions, and latent soulish battles.

I asked my mentor (who by this time was in his mid-70s) if he still struggled with matters of the flesh, such as temptation, lust, envy, jealousy, fear, doubt, disobedience, carnal desires, anger, rage, and selfishness.

His answer was a resounding "yes!"

I was young in the Lord and barely entering ministry. Still, his answer revolutionized my devotion to always be full of Holy Ghost fire lest I end up cold and indifferent towards my Lord and God!

The Battle of Prayer

The battle of every servant of God will be one of intense seeking after God. I don't say this lightly or nonchalantly. If the soldier of Jesus is to survive in the battle to please God with the tasks given or to overcome self and sin, one must always remain prostrated before God.

My pastor told me after meeting for early prayer one morning: *David, the Lord showed me that if we are to advance in the battle and take the enemies' camp, we must crawl and inch our way forward. Don't dare to stand up and run, or you will get shot! We must learn to crawl if we want to advance!*

At another holy moment, while in early morning prayer with my pastor, as we labored in fervent prayer and intercession, I quieted myself to hear my pastor praying at the altar. His prayer continued: *"Lord, I don't want to be anybody big! Just make me a buck private in your army. I'll go and do anything you ask of me. Please, Lord, don't let me be anything big!"*

If You Fall in a Battle!

There will be many battles in the war for the souls of lost humanity. Yes, you heard me correctly; there are many battles! Some battles will be easy to overcome; other battles will be very challenging, and others will be lost.

What do you do as a soldier who has been shot? You get back up, and you keep walking. You shake yourself, get restored, healed, or under someone's care until you are ready to keep fighting. The point is that there are many battles in a war. The war is not over until it is over! Keep fighting till the war ends! If you fall, get back up – the war has not ended! Arise in the Name of Jesus! I say arise!

My friends, I have reached the end of this manuscript, and my heart yearns for nothing more than for these notes to set your life ablaze. May your heart burn with holy passion and enter the reality that says, *"He must increase, but I must decrease!"*

For More Books

by

David Mayorga

go to

www.shabarpublications.com

mayorga1126@gmail.com